Published and distributed by

ISLAND HERITAGE
P U B L I S H I N G

99-880 IWAENA STREET, AIEA, HAWAII 96701-3202
PHONE: (808) 487-7299 • Fax: (808) 488-2279
EMAIL: hawaii4u@pixi.com

ISBN 0-89610-002-2
First Edition, First Printing - 1998

# THE UGLY 'ELEPAIO

Written & Illustrated by Tammy Yee

ISLAND HERITAGE

Dedication:

*For Cosmo, my eager fledgling*

Deep in a Hawaiian rain forest as old as time there stood a tall and ancient ʻōhiʻa lehua tree. The tree was a favorite among the birds of the forest. Its silvery branches were lush and sturdy. Its red blossoms were bountiful and heavy with sweet and fragrant nectar.

One spring, two 'elepaio came and made a nest in the 'ōhi'a tree. It was a small and tidy nest, woven with care and lined with the finest spider's silk. Mama 'Elepaio laid a single white egg with reddish brown freckles on one end. Then Mama and Papa 'Elepaio took turns sitting in the nest, keeping their precious egg safe and warm.

As the days stretched into weeks, Papa 'Elepaio grew worried.

"Mama," he softly chirped, "summer is already here. I don't think our little egg will hatch."

"Oh, Papa, just a little while longer. Give our keiki a chance," cried Mama 'Elepaio.

Papa did not have the heart to say no.

"We can sit for one more night, Mama," he said. "In the morning we must leave."

That night, a storm swept over the rain forest. Gusts rattled the branches of the 'ōhi'a tree and sent leaves swirling through the night. Cold rain pelted down through the canopy. The 'ōhi'a tree swayed in the wind but stood strong.

Mama and Papa 'Elepaio huddled together in their tiny nest.

By morning, the storm had passed. Mama 'Elepaio shook the rain from her feathers, then stood to check on her egg.

"Keet! Keet! Keet!" she cried, hopping from branch to branch. "Papa, our egg is gone!"

Papa and Mama searched the tree from its highest branches to the ground. They could find no sign of their egg. Mama had just about given up hope when Papa noticed a trembling 'ōhi'a leaf caught in the fork of a branch. He turned over the leaf and let out an alarming "Wheet!"

"Mama! Mama! Come and look!" chittered Papa ʻElepaio. Beneath the leaf was a tiny chick, wet and shivering. Its skin was bright orange-pink. It had matted gray down above each eye and on top of its head. And when he opened his mouth, auwē! The inside of his gaping mouth was rosy pink with a touch of orange! The ʻElepaios had never seen anything like it.

Mama ʻElepaio peered up into the canopy.

"Poor baby, the wind must have knocked him from his nest. Please, Papa, we must hānai him," pleaded Mama.

"I don't think he will live," warned Papa. "He looks awful."

"No, Papa," smiled Mama as she cradled the chick in the fold of her wings. "He looks beautiful."

The ʻElepaios loved the little chick as if it were their own. They named him Liko, after the budding leaves of the ʻōhiʻa tree.

At first Liko lost weight and was terribly ill. Mama and Papa never left his side. They cared for him day and night, feeding him, cleaning him, and keeping him warm and dry.

Liko grew stronger day by day. His downy feathers grew thick and fluffy, and his appetite improved. The little chick loved big and juicy caterpillars. With his mouth wide open, he was always begging for more. More, more, more. More caterpillars, please!

And his cry! Liko would squeak and gurgle and creak like a rusty door hinge! Not at all like the dainty chirp and chatter of an ʻelepaio chick. But Mama and Papa ʻElepaio thought it was the most beautiful song they had ever heard.

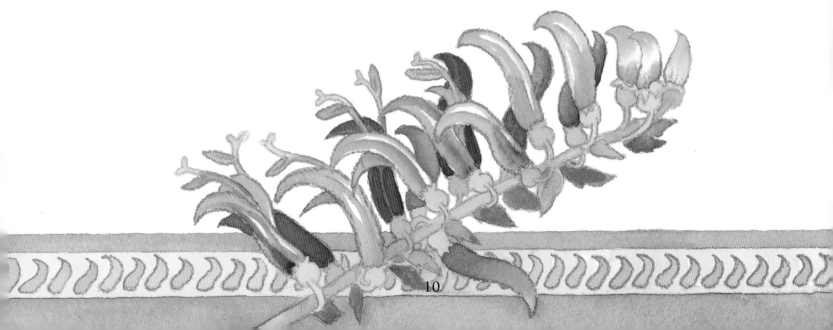

When it became apparent that Liko would survive, Papa decided it was time to make a birth announcement. He fluttered from branch to branch with his black tail held high, singing "Chee-WHEE-o!"

Birds from all over the rain forest gathered to see what the excitement was about . . . yellow-green 'amakihi, gray 'ōma'o, and a meddlesome brown 'elepaio named Niele. They landed near where Mama 'Elepaio nestled with her downy chick.

"Tseet! Tseet!" whistled the 'amakihi. "Why do you sing, 'Elepaio?"

Papa 'Elepaio puffed up his chest. "Keet! Keet! A keiki! Mama and I have a keiki!" he called.

"And have you named him?" asked the 'amakihi.

"Why, yes," answered Mama 'Elepaio. "We call him Liko."

The forest birds began to chatter noisily. To name a nestling and announce its birth was a very, very special occasion. It meant that the chick was strong and healthy. So many chicks in the forest succumbed to the cold, or to sickness.

"What a beautiful name," the 'ōma'o sang sweetly. The other birds agreed. Liko was a name that sang of hope and promise.

13

"Where is he, where is he?" chirped Niele 'Elepaio. She was called Niele because she was always poking her beak into other birds' business.

Niele hopped closer to the nest and tried to peer in. But Mama 'Elepaio was very protective and she sat firmly on her chick.

"You should use more lichen and spider webs," scolded Niele as she inspected the nest. "This nest will never hold together!"

Peck, peck, peck! Niele pecked rudely at the nest's lining.

Pop! Out from the nest poked a little head, all orange and fuzzy with gray down on top!

"Sque-e-eak!" piped a frightened Liko.

Niele fell off the tree and into a patch of ferns. She was quite embarrassed, and quite angry. The other forest birds were startled. They flapped away to nearby branches, where they sat squabbling and squawking. *What kind of chick is that? Did you see that big beak of his? And that awful color!*

Then away they flew, teasing,
"Liko, Liko,
Hear him squeak
Oh, the ugly 'elepaio!

His beak so long,
That awful song!
He's the ugly 'elepaio!"

Poor little Liko.  All he could do was squeak
sadly as his mother held him close.
"Never mind what they say," she soothed.
"They're just jealous."
Liko was a lonely little chick. Sometimes
other fledglings would come to play.  To them,
Liko was just like any other chick.  They did not
care if he were red, or blue, or green.   But their
parents would always swoop down to chase them
back home.  They would never allow their keiki to play
with such an ugly creature!

Mama 'Elepaio would sometimes call him Lele Ua, for he was a precious gift of the windblown rain. Lele also meant "to jump" or "to hop." And Liko certainly was a bubbly little fledgling! He would perch on the edge of the nest on his wobbly orange legs and fidget. Bounce, bounce, bounce. Hop, hop, hop. He simply could not sit still!

"Be patient, my little Liko, my Lele Ua, for one day you will blossom like the lehua in the highest branches," Mama 'Elepaio would always sing.

As the weeks passed, Liko's gray and white down was replaced by yellow-green feathers speckled with black. His beak had grown long and curved, and looked ridiculously big for his little body.

One day, as he hopped from branch to branch, Liko spied a beautiful red 'ōhi'a blossom on a far limb. He hopped and hopped but could not reach it. Oh, how he wanted that flower! Leaning out over the nearest branch, he stretched and he stretched and...

Wheeee!  Little Liko found himself flying!  Flap, flap, flap!  All over
the 'ōhi'a tree!

Zooom!  Down over the other fledglings he swooped, scattering
them through the trees.  And such a noisy flier was he!

The other birds would shriek, "Aī, what is that awful flutter?
It sounds like a bat!"

Mama and Papa 'Elepaio were so proud.

20

Now Liko could visit every blossom in the forest. And he found that with his long beak, he could easily sip a flower's sweet nectar. What a special beak he had!

The other birds became quite envious.

It was time for Liko to leave the nest. Papa wiped a stray tear from his eye as he waved good-bye. But Liko promised that he would always come back to visit.

Before long, summer was over. Autumn passed into winter, and winter came and went like a tropical storm. The rain forest thrived in the cool, wet weather.

Spring returned, and soon the misty forest was filled with the chorus of chirping birds readying themselves for the nesting season.

All except for Liko. Poor Liko still felt that he was too ugly for anyone's company.

Early one morning, as Liko perched on a mossy limb, he beheld a beautiful red bird high up in the canopy. He had never seen a bird so lovely. She was scarlet with pretty black wings and a black tail. She had a long, graceful, salmon-colored beak, which she would delicately dip into the flowers.

Liko was too shy to approach. He hid behind some wet 'ōhi'a leaves and watched her from afar. But the leaves around him began to rustle with his nervous fidgeting.

"Who is it?" asked the pretty red bird as she tilted her head in Liko's direction. She flew over to his hiding spot and peeked in.

"Hello," she squeaked. "My name is Lehua. What's yours?"

Liko was speechless. The rusty creak of her song was music to his ears! And her noisy flapping was like the pitter-patter of his racing heart!

24

"M-my name is Liko," he stammered. "But I don't think you want to talk to me."

"Why not?" asked Lehua.

"Because I'm ugly," he answered.

Lehua giggled. Liko thought she was laughing at his ugliness, and he drew further back into the leaves.

"Oh, sweet Liko, your feathers are redder than the reddest blossom, your wings darker than the darkest lava," sang Lehua. "You are the most beautiful 'i'iwi I have ever seen."

Liko gazed down at his reflection in the rain-slicked leaves. Instead of a speckled bird with a big beak, he saw a brilliant red bird with a beak as bright as sunrise! No longer was he an ugly 'elepaio. He was an 'i'iwi!

He fluttered from branch to branch, flicking his black tail and warbling noisily like a rusty harmonica. Hop, hop, hop. Squeak, squawk, squeak. Who would have thought that he would grow into such a beautiful bird!

"'I'iwi!  'I'iwi!  I'm an 'i'iwi!" he rejoiced.

Lehua was puzzled.  Liko behaved so strangely, just like a...

Just like a giddy 'elepaio!  He was so unusual, so special.  It made Lehua love him even more.

Liko had finally found himself.  And he found love.

29

Together, Liko and Lehua flew off in search of an 'ōhi'a tree.
An 'ōhi'a tree, strong and tall, to build a nest in its silvery branches.
By summer, they had two little chicks of their very own, with
orange-pink skin, big beaks and gray down above each eye.

And Mama and Papa 'Elepaio visited every day, bringing big and juicy caterpillars for their grandchildren. The little chicks would squeak and squawk with their beaks wide open, calling for more. More, more, more. More caterpillars, please!

So if one day you journey through Hawai'i's rain forests, and you see a flock of 'i'iwis behaving strangely, stay a while and watch. If they hop from branch to branch with their tails cocked high, like 'elepaios, then you have found Liko and his family. Liko, the ugly 'elepaio who blossomed like the beautiful lehua in the highest branches!

# GLOSSARY

**ʻAmakihi**  This yellow-green bird feeds on insects, nectar and fruits in Hawaiʻi's native forests.

**ʻElepaio**  A perky and curious bird, the brown ʻelepaio is known as the guardian spirit of Hawaiian canoe builders.

**Hānai**  To nourish or feed.

**ʻIʻiwi**  Young ʻiʻiwi are splotchy yellow-green with black spots. In time, the young birds mature into beautiful scarlet birds with salmon-colored beaks. ʻIʻiwi use their long, curved beaks to feed on nectar.

**Keiki**  Child

**Lehua**  The brushy flower of the ʻōhiʻa tree.

**ʻŌhiʻa**  The first tree to grow on lava flows, ʻōhiʻa is the most common tree in Hawaiʻi's native rain forests. Its beautiful blossoms provide nectar for many of the forest's birds and insects.

**ʻŌmaʻo**  Follow the melodious song of the gray ʻōmaʻo, and you may find it feeding on its favorite foods—fruits, berries and insects.